Shooting Galler

®©

Written by Scott Wozniak

Illustrated by Andrew Nutini

ALIEN BUDDHA PRESS 2019

The presence of Scott Wozniak in the small press grows in stature with every published poem of his. Wozniak is a poet who has lived and survived through times so desperate, bleak and hopeless, he is a poet that brings a force of such stark imagery that it'll bolt you to your chair. Wozniak is a poet who has died, many times, like those around him, but at the last moment he has crawled from the gripping of darkness and lived on to write it down and Wozniak writes it down damn good, clean and with a surging clarity that makes it come to life as if you were witness to the event, and that is just one of Wozniak's qualities.

Throughout this book Wozniak displays an open and endless sense of compassion, sometimes it feels very distant, but it is there and so is his lively and spiked sense of humour that will take you by surprise like a pouncing Jaguar. A majority of the poems hit me straight-off, far too many to mention here, but here are a few: 'Normal is what You Make It' 'Exchange Rate' 'Even The Worst Laid Plans' 'Expensive Beer' 'Not All Ignorance is Bliss' 'Bloody Gashes' 'Show Me An Option' 'Sunday Morning Mass' 'Miracle In Action' 'Not Your Average Wino' 'A Sorry Excuse for Suicide'

Wozniak's reflections are harsh and harrowing. These poems are in your streets, in your town, Wozniak has now brought them into a public space. Andrew Nutini's illustrations do not simply accompany, enhance and envelope the poems. They could easily be stand alone pieces, the work is finely tuned with an undercurrent that elegantly mirrors the tone, movement and atmosphere of the poem. Initially the illustrations may pull you away from the words, demanding your attention for exploration but, ultimately, the illustrations become the poems and vice-versa, so that you cannot imagine one without the other:

Several times during the reading of this book, in between poems, I thought of the Art Pepper: 'Notes of A Jazz Survivor' documentary; a testament of strength and character, of facing down demons and producing extraordinary works of creativity exploring the human condition. Wozniak is here with this book and this book will be one of the strongest collections you have ever read. Buy this book and find out for yourself.

John D Robinson

Holy&intoxicated Publications UK.

The author would like to thank and acknowledge the following presses where some of these poems were first published: Paper and Ink Literary Zine, Midnight Lane Boutique, Mad Swirl, Walking Is Still Honest, Svensk Apache Press, and 48th Street Press.

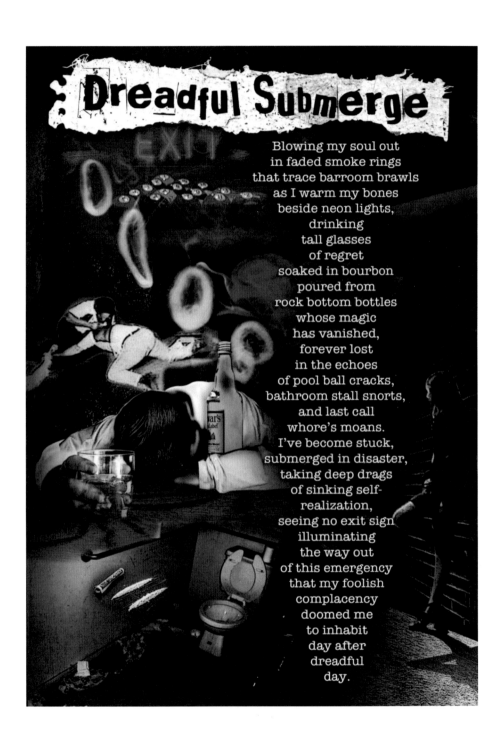

Dreadful Submerge

Blowing my soul out
in faded smoke rings
that trace barroom brawls
as I warm my bones
beside neon lights,
drinking
tall glasses
of regret
soaked in bourbon
poured from
rock bottom bottles
whose magic
has vanished,
forever lost
in the echoes
of pool ball cracks,
bathroom stall snorts,
and last call
whore's moans.
I've become stuck,
submerged in disaster,
taking deep drags
of sinking self-
realization,
seeing no exit sign
illuminating
the way out
of this emergency
that my foolish
complacency
doomed me
to inhabit
day after
dreadful
day.

Blindingly Obvious

If pain
is inconsequential,
if fear
is inconsequential,
why do repercussions
of living
entrenched
in both
manifest
themselves
so blatantly
in the lives
we begrudgingly
endure?

A Risky Mark

Walking
in the ghetto
alone, caring
about nothing
but a fix
may be dangerous,
but when demonic
orchestras
are composing
anguish
on decomposing
bones,
even the blind
can see
you'll take them
to hell
with you
if that's
all it takes
to silence
this symphony
of discord.

Normal is What You Make It

How has this
become
normal?

Normal
people
are afraid
of needles.

Normal
people
don't go
walking
through
ghettos
alone
at night.

Normal
people
have
a conscience

that stops them
from stealing
to feed
the thing
killing them.
Normal people
don't
grab a spoon
from a drawer
and leave
everything
behind.

Caring only
for blood
mixing
with a dark
swirl
of oppression
at the bottom
of a dirty
syringe.

eXchange Rate

Imagine all the
exotic locations
money goes

What ya got?
$20 spot.
-Panties drop-

What ya got?
$20 spot.
-Crack rock-

Destined to
end up in
the hood.

Deadly Exotic

You are an exotic,
carnivorous plant
that grows
from a pile
of trash.

A man-eating
perennial
popping up
from the filth
in the gutter.

I've watched
how you devour,
it's hypnotic
to witness
your assault.

Poor bastards,
if they only knew
your beauty
is nothing
but bait.

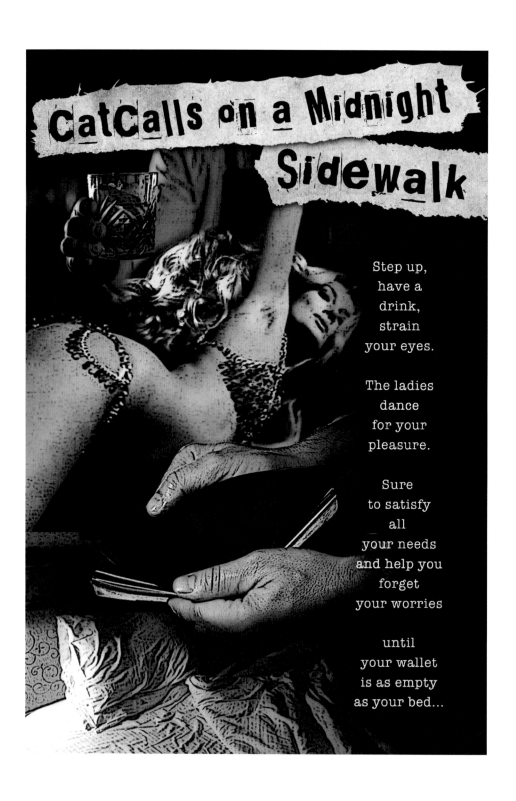

CatCalls on a Midnight Sidewalk

Step up,
have a
drink,
strain
your eyes.

The ladies
dance
for your
pleasure.

Sure
to satisfy
all
your needs
and help you
forget
your worries

until
your wallet
is as empty
as your bed...

DeAth's Metamorphosis

Immortality
is a luxury
of the young.

As time passes
and age lurches
forward,
launching us
ever closer
to our graves,
we are forced
to face
the demons
from our pasts.

The ones
we thought
we overcame
will always find
a way
to drag us
down

in the dirt
by putting
a new face
on our past
transgressions.

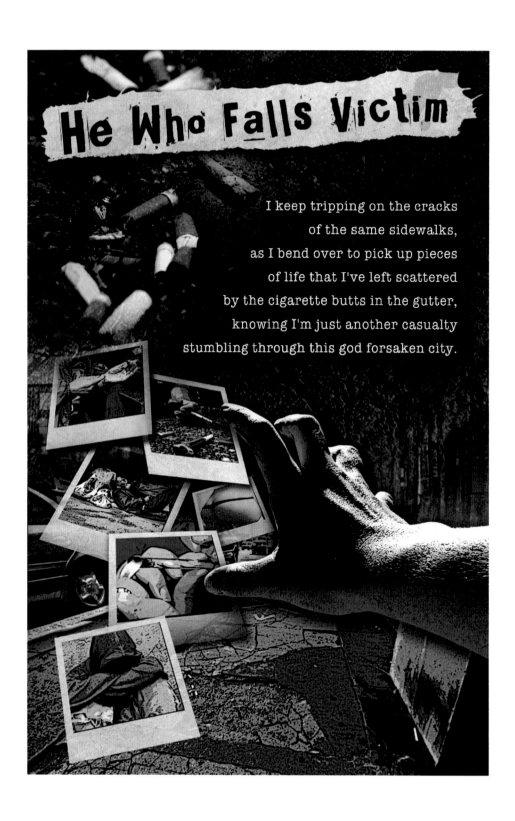

He Who Falls Victim

I keep tripping on the cracks
of the same sidewalks,
as I bend over to pick up pieces
of life that I've left scattered
by the cigarette butts in the gutter,
knowing I'm just another casualty
stumbling through this god forsaken city.

Dandy Predator

His cane
has a wolf's head
carved
in the handle.

He stalks his way
up the streets.

A proper dandy
predator
he thinks he is.

A Clockwork Orange
his inspiration
for living;
just the first half,
he disregards the second.

Strange for a guy
with three strikes,
labeled
career criminal,
who's gone through
multiple rounds
of reprogramming
by the state.

Guess it didn't take.

Even the Worst Laid Plans

No good
could come of it.

This was as plain
to see
as the rig
in my arm.

We'd hatched
a plan:

Get black
fishing vests
that look like
bulletproofs,
handguns,
and those D.E.A.
shirts and hats
they sell
at the corner.

Take Osh's
police auction
Crown Vic
and head down
to the dope spot
on West Side Ave.

where they got
that bomb shit
and 15-year-old kids
running it.

We hopped the curb,
jumped out the car
with guns drawn,
screamed,
"Get the FUCK down
on the ground, NOW!"
Grabbed the ones
who didn't run,
slammed 'em
on the ground,
stepped on necks,
went through pockets,
grabbed dope,
and got the fuck out
while they were praying
not to go to county.

I never thought
it would work,
but not one shot
was fired
till we got home
and tied off.

Jackpot on the Dumpster Diver Circuit

I walk around
the city
wearing rags
that smell
like bum,
looking
for anything
nobody wants,
but I need.

I search every
dumpster
and trash can
crossing
my path.

A half-eaten
burrito
is top score
until
I toss open
a lid
and see
abandoned
Doc Martins—
a possession
I could
never afford,
but are now
all mine
for the low,
low price
of homeless.

Kids These Days Got It Too Easy

Whatever happened
to good ol'
crack n' heroin?

Kids these days
are getting high
on Spice,
kratum,
and any number
of pharmaceuticals.

All shit
that can be acquired
at head shops
or from doctors,
away from the threat
of having a gun
shoved
in your face.

This reality
scares me
more
than the time
I was put on my knees

with a gun pressed
to the back
of my head
in a drug deal
gone bad.

If you never
see the ugly
side of drugs,
how the fuck
will you ever
want to quit?

Then again,
none of the 3 am
ghetto
scavenger hunts
motivated me
to stop.

I wonder
if they've got
a pill
for that?

Any Place but Here

Malt liquor
breakfast,
street corner
hustle,
alleyway
injection,
bushes
to sleep in.

These are days
when hell
seems
like a nice place
to warm
your bones.

Unfortunately,
THEY won't even
let you in,
even though
you smell
like death.

As DeAth Begs

Death is sitting
on the sidewalk
against a storefront-
knees pulled up,
head sagging,
arms outstretched,
hands cupped,
begging for change.

He's dressed
like a bum
I see there
daily.

Not one person
in this city
has noticed
as they walk by,
except me.

And I'm too busy
chasing chiva
(Death's cheap catalyst)
out the pockets
of Mexicans
to give a shit,
either.

The Price of Full-Tilt Living

Everything comes
at a cost.

I'm not very good
at determining price.

Seems I overpay
more than I ought to.

If you can't
spot the mark
when sitting
at the table,
it's best
to walk away—
it's probably
you.

The Gods
have emptied
my pockets
and now I'm playing
get-back.

It's never good
to continue
on tilt.

Not All Ignorance is Bliss

Head tilted
toward sky,
eyes wide
and bulging,
jaw unhinged,
waiting.

It happened
almost
on command.

Like a volcano
spewing blood
and Budweiser.

Then, it was over
as suddenly
as it occurred.
He wiped his mouth
with his shirt,
rubbed the tears
from his eyes,
and mumbled,

"Damn, this ulcer
is killing me,"
then cracked
another beer
for good measure.

Losing

I once heard
a man say,
"Though I've never
been broken,
I too
know how to
pick up the pieces."

He tells me this
as I'm sitting
in rehab
for the third time
in two years,
trying to fix
a scattered
jigsaw mess.

I can't trust
a man
who's never destroyed
something he loves,
he doesn't know
how to reconstruct
himself
out of aftermath.

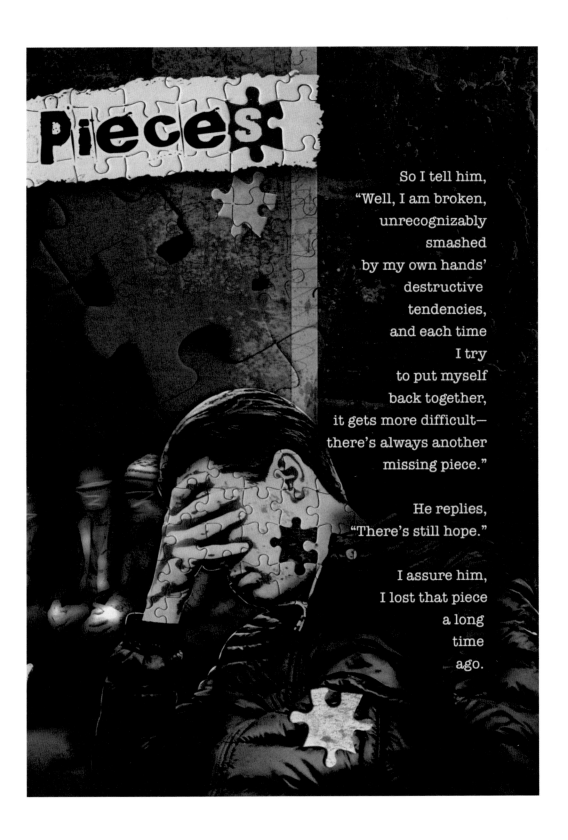

Pieces

So I tell him,
"Well, I am broken,
unrecognizably
smashed
by my own hands'
destructive
tendencies,
and each time
I try
to put myself
back together,
it gets more difficult—
there's always another
missing piece."

He replies,
"There's still hope."

I assure him,
I lost that piece
a long
time
ago.

An Allergic Reaction

One long blur
of blacked-out nights
and hellish mornings.

My good-time
intentions
always get
out of hand.

The more I come to
on jailhouse floors,
the more clear
it becomes--
I have an allergic
reaction
to booze.

I break out
in handcuffs
and felonies.

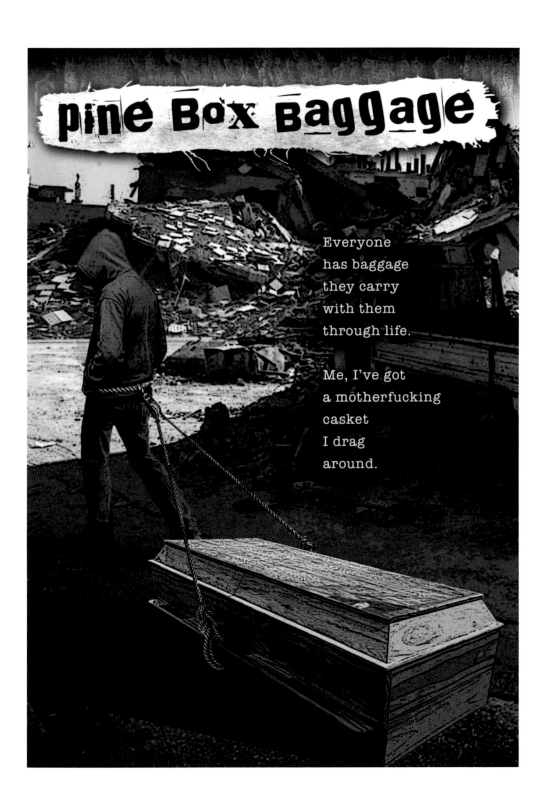

pine Box Baggage

Everyone
has baggage
they carry
with them
through life.

Me, I've got
a motherfucking
casket
I drag
around.

Cleaning Streets
with Spilt Blood

Strung-out
street kids
celebrate.

At 3 am
their squat's
door
is kicked in
by hired
guns.

They scream,
plea,
cry,
and run.

All that will
be found
is two bodies,
empty
9mm rounds,
and another
reason
to scream,
"Fuck the Police!"

28

Bloody Gashes

She was reading
a chapter titled,
"Profuse Vaginal
Bleeding."

It made me think
about our hidden
bloody gashes.

Gashes
of the past
that left scars
even though
the bleeding
never stopped.

Gashes
we accept
as part of us.

Bloody gashes,
dripping, oozing,
staining the people
we dare hold dear.

I'm glad I have you
to compare gashes
with.

Most people
go through life
all alone,
bleeding in secret.

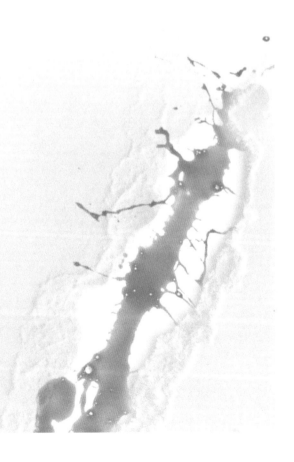

Smoke, Bugout, Repeat

Piss sink hotel
crack stem dead end

Sirens sound
neighbors shout

Pipe gets lit
eyes bug out

You tell yourself
just one more hit

Gambling with Counterfeit Bills

Fully invested
in our lives,
and placing bets
with bad luck
currency.

The cards we hold
get laid down
with little thought.

Our best intentions
are given
minor attention.

It's the thrill
of the ride
motivating
the stakes.

Over time
they get higher,
and our habits
force us
to go all in
more often
than we'd like.

Together We Are Separate

We sleep en mass,
yet rarely together.
Huddled lumps
of humanity
curled up
under bridges
in scratchy, gray wool
food bank blankets.

We're familiar
with one another
but separate.

We know faces
and names
but not the person.

There's a bottle passed
but no history.

Backstories unnecessary,
reasons irrelevant,
the effect
more important
than the cause.

The only comfort
we share.

Time to Scatter

Everyone
in the house
was on the run
from a different
state
and lived
off criminal
activity.

It was noon,
there was a knock
at the door
as the bodies
leftover
from a rowdy night
slept it off
while Eddie
was tending
to plants
in the attic.

At one point
in the night
we watched
Crime Stoppers,
which showed footage
from a bank robbery.

We knew
the guy hiding
behind a hat
and dark shades
looked familiar
but weren't sure how
until the Feds
at the door,
holding
a picture
of the man
responsible,
asked
if we knew Craig.

That explained
why he hadn't
been home
in 3 days,
but it didn't
explain
how the fuck
they knew
he lived
with us.

Show Me an Option
(for the Reverend)

Two kids
and a wife
who need
the money
brought in
by illicit
sales
of false hope.

He wants
to quit,
knows
his habit
is slow death.

But who can go
to rehab
for sixty days
when there's
bills to pay
and three mouths
to feed?

It's not about
getting high,
it's about
responsibilities.

Wrestling with Ghosts

Eyes bulging from skull,
a three-day cocaine rage
pumping through his arteries.
He sits at the bar
in conversation
with the hallucination
of a long-dead friend.

The couple
three stools down
think he's insane—
they're watching him
carefully, not wanting
to draw attention
to themselves.

Little do they know
this is normal
Wednesday behavior.
Come back Friday night
and they'll see
the real show,
where he and the ghost
reenact the knife fight.

It's a weekly
occurrence.

Only Kidding Ourselves

Neon junkies,
street corner
stompers,
fast-lane racers,
and bail jumpers,
all livin' life
in dead man's rags.

With kicks
or a fix,
we're all lookin'
for the same thing—
that moment
where we forget
EVERYTHING.

All the while,
we know
our only peace
will be found
in sixpence
on eyelids.

Curbside Angels

Curbside angels
with broken wings
beg for smokes
and some spare change.

With just one fix
they'll fly away.

Want for Nothing

A feral pack
of dirty kids
attack a case
of Beast Ice
bought
with spare change,
piercing cans
with church-keys
to ensure
speedy
consumption.

Aside from this
and the prospect
of a dumpster
full of food,
nothing
fucking
matters.

Not All Rides are Good Rides

Three road dogs
coated
in highway grime
and Jim Beam stench
stand with thumbs
in the wind.

A tweaked out,
eighteen-wheel,
redneck savior
pulls his rig over.

Three miles
down the road
he pulls
a .38 revolver
with duct tape grip
from under his ass.

Knives
flick open,
signaling the man
to stop.

No Need for Chicken-Shit bank Robbers

Someday
Dog Day Afternoon
will become reality,
banks will be robbed
and I won't
be full of shit,
claiming I want
to bring down
the institutions.

I'll have a shotgun,
a bag of cash,
a few hostages,
and no way out.

I'll probably
piss my pants
while screaming
like a madman
fulfilling dreams.

But then again,
I'll probably
remain
full of shit,
like everyone
else.

Looking for Scars with Blinders On

At the age
of fifteen
she found her first
boyfriend dead
from an overdose
in the van
they lived in.

Every boyfriend after
was an addict,
they all cheated on her
with lovers
that took the shape
of powders.

Lying
and sneaking
behind her back
to chase
the dragon's ass.

If you ask her,
none of it left scars,
her life hasn't
been traumatic,
just normal shit
all kids deal with.

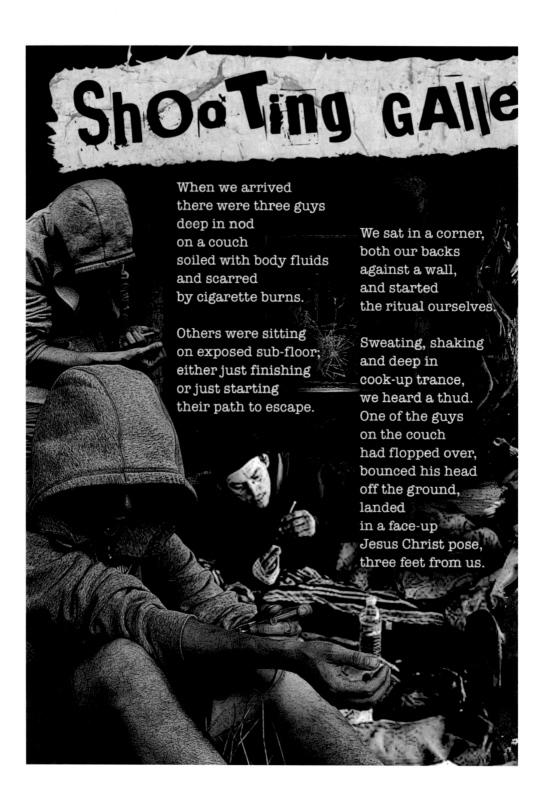

ShOoTing GAlle

When we arrived
there were three guys
deep in nod
on a couch
soiled with body fluids
and scarred
by cigarette burns.

Others were sitting
on exposed sub-floor;
either just finishing
or just starting
their path to escape.

We sat in a corner,
both our backs
against a wall,
and started
the ritual ourselves.

Sweating, shaking
and deep in
cook-up trance,
we heard a thud.
One of the guys
on the couch
had flopped over,
bounced his head
off the ground,
landed
in a face-up
Jesus Christ pose,
three feet from us.

VULTUrEs

Craig and I looked
at each other,
wondering what to do.
A few of the others
got up
and walked over
to the guy.

When they started going
through his pockets
instead of giving CPR
or checking for a pulse
we decided to pack up
and get high behind
the 7-11 dumpster.

It's bad mojo
to get loaded
by a dead body,
especially
when the vultures
are circling.

Bay Area Welcome Wagon

I hadn't been
in San Fran
for a year.

I was back
for less
than an hour,
walking down
the sidewalk
in front
of Fred's Market.

I saw a guy
in the street
making a scene—
yelling at drivers
and waving his arms
while jaywalking
through traffic.

He slapped
the hood
of a car,
stepped over

the curb,
and walked up
to me
while removing
his hat
and flashing
a badge,
then threw me
against the wall
and started digging
in my pockets.

"Hey bud, where ya been,
on vacation?"

"Fuck you, Goff!"

He figured out
I wasn't holding.

I figured out
some pigs
have the memory
of elephants.

the sAme Ol' UpHill BattLe

Destined
to eternally
push
his cart
from trash can
to trash can,
searching
for aluminum
cans
he can trade
for cash
that gets him
a can or two
of beer
to drink
while pushing
his cart
full of cans
around town,
on the hunt
for more cans
to trade
for more beer.

He's a drunk
Sisyphus
with a
shopping-cart.

Don't Give a Bad Cop Good Ideas

I'd been
passed out drunk
for who-knows-how-long
in some bushes
outside
an emergency room
in New Orleans
when I was kicked
in the ribs.

I sat up swinging
the mag light
I kept hidden
up my sleeve.

When I realized
it was a cop
I diverted
it's trajectory.

He didn't notice,
just told me
I couldn't sleep there,

and to find
a well hid spot,
cause if he found me again,
he'd kick my ass.
If his cronies
hadn't come
to the squat
two nights earlier
to shoot street kids,
I'd have been there;
out of sight
from public eyes.

I wanted
to tell him this,
but figured
it best to not
put ideas
in his head.

Lucky to Have Your Pants

Raised on streets,
schooled in the ways
of the Artful Dodger.

Beauty makes her
seem vulnerable,
but you're the prey.

While your pants
are around ankles,
one hand
is on your balls,
the other,
on your wallet.

Before you can moan
she's out the door,
down the block
counting her score.

CaN't Argue facTS

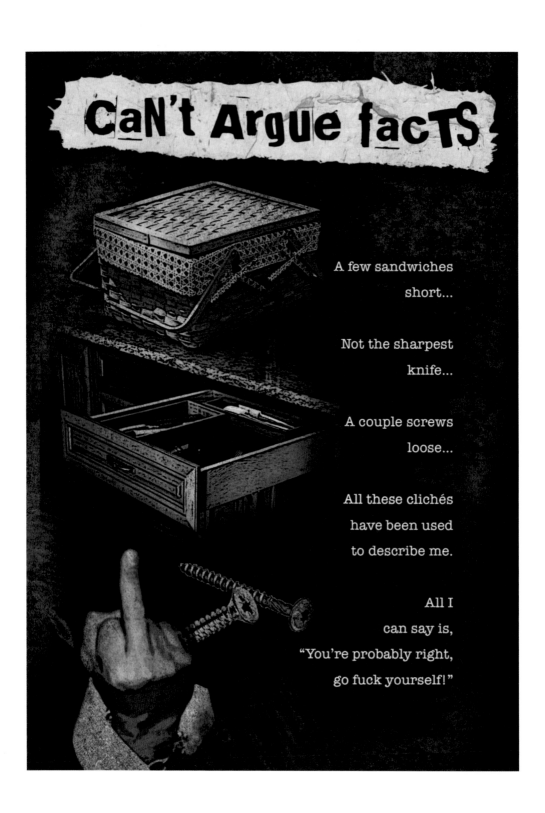

A few sandwiches short...

Not the sharpest knife...

A couple screws loose...

All these clichés have been used to describe me.

All I can say is, "You're probably right, go fuck yourself!"

Sunday Morning Mass

Early Sunday morning
I needed a fix, so
I hopped the El
to the west side
and walked to K-town.

Until that moment,
it never registered
they'd been hustling
in front a church.

It was 9 am
and only the sound
of an organ
and folks
in their Sunday best
were on the corner.

My dumb, junky ass
got die-motherfucker-looks
from the elder ladies
of the church,
and I figured
I should search
elsewhere.

The neighborhood
was dead,
I'd forgot
most black folks
worship God
instead of blaming.

I walked around,
searching
for salvation
while getting sicker
by the minute.

Eventually,
it was business
as usual—
Kids hustling
outside the church
their grandmama
praised Jesus in,
and me climbing
in a back-alley dumpster
with a bag of dope,
on my way to meet God
the only way I know.

Miracle in Action

Anyone
who says
you can't
raise the dead
has obviously
never
had the pleasure
of shoving ice
up the butt
of a guy
over-dosing.

That dead
bastard's eyes
will pop open
so fast
you'll have to explain
why your hand
is up his ass.

Driving in Darkness

We were driving around
the wrong neighborhood,
at the wrong hour,
looking for things
to do wrong with.

A couple guys
walking
down the road
took advantage
of our bad decisions
by pulling a gun
and taking our cash.

Afterward,
my boy calmly drove
around the block, then
as we re-approached,
jumped the sidewalk,
killed the lights,
and mowed them over—
our car bouncing
over bodies
like speed bumps—

flicked the lights on,
pulled back on the road
and kept going
like nothing happened.
I just laughed
as we drove further
into darkness.

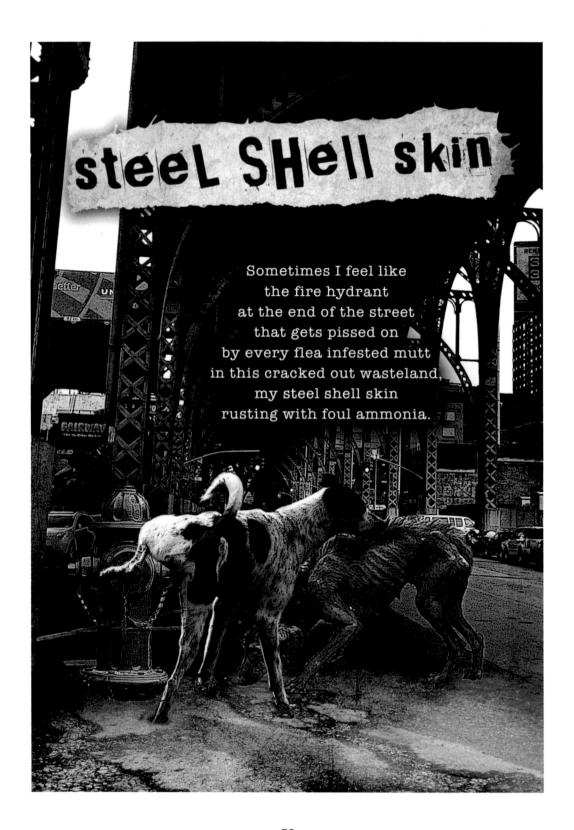

steeL SHell skin

Sometimes I feel like
the fire hydrant
at the end of the street
that gets pissed on
by every flea infested mutt
in this cracked out wasteland,
my steel shell skin
rusting with foul ammonia.

On the Backs of History

We've built
our lives
on backs
that refuse
to support
our dreams.

The centuries
underneath
these cities
wait for us
to crumble.

We walk
on bones,
laughing
with ill-deserved
arrogance.

Our future
is a corpse
decomposing
with rash
decisions.

Taking Blasts at Innocence

The poison
gets inside
by riding
on the backs
of demons
that perch
in our brain,
secreting toxins
that flow
thru bloodstreams
in veins
leading
to our heart.

Once things
are black enough,
the poison
spreads
to your soul.

We feel it happen,
but excuse it
for dread,
turmoil,
or suffering.

Once the demon
is inside us,
it's too late,
fate sealed,
hope forsaken,
insanity norm,
reactions
involuntary,
actions
justified,
dog
eat
dog
is the mantra
whispered
over
and
over
inside our skulls.

A heavy hand
and empty heart
are left
to fulfill the work
of vacancy.

You can't blame
Moloch
when it's you
who pulled
the trigger.

Not your Average Wino

for Wayne-o

A Black Velvet bottle,
rolling tobacco tin,
Carlo Rossi jug,
two church keys,
and freight train
memorabilia
decorated
his headstone.

I was two days late
for the funeral.......

I sat
on the ground
with a twelve-pack
of Milwaukee's Best,
cussed, cried,
and said cheers
while drinking
my half.

Every time
I cracked
a fresh beer,
I'd bury one
deep
in fresh dirt.

As I shoved
the last one
in the ground,
my arm buried
to the shoulder
in his grave,
cold dirt kissing
my cheek,
I heard a train whistle
and knew
it was him
telling me
to get off
the fucking
tracks.

Orchestral Madness

The city conducts
its song
as I'm highlighted
by street lights
and searching cracks
for a resting place
where I can lay
and listen
to the orchestral
madness
riding on winds
that transform
chaos
into music
gently rocking me
to sleep
on concrete
sheets.

Living on Scraps

Living
gutter
denizens
giving up
on divinity
and accepting
life
as hell
find food
in trashcans
as your stomach
swells.

But what
the fuck
do you care?

You got yours.

PeASAnt kiNg in rAgs

Partying
in an alley
off 4th Ave
for 40 ounces'
birthday.

Everyone
pitched in
money made
panhandling
to celebrate
by getting
extra
shitfaced.

Jim Beam,
Carlo Rossi,
King Cobra,
and lice
were shared
in abundance.

His gift from us all,
a stolen shopping-cart,
was stashed
behind a dumpster.

As it was rolled
out of hiding
we sang
Happy Birthday
and poured beer
over his head.

With a broke-
tooth-grin,
he grabbed
the handle
of the cart,
put two 40's in it,
and pushed his way
down the dark
sidewalk
like he was king
of the world.

UNDERPASS
DO NOT ENTER
WHEN
FLOODED

Missing the Target

All us bastards
are here
at the bottom
for reasons
we'd rather
forget.

Our individual,
self-inflicted,
prisons of choice
make it possible
for us
to endure
this hellish
existence
with no
recollection
of today.

Relief in the Shape of Doom

Dancing girls,
with purses full
of dick-tease-tips
walk by
as I try to stay dry
by standing
in a doorway
while waiting
for a guy
with lying eyes
who told me
he could remove
my pain.

I'm stuck
watching cops
watch me
as they drive
the block.

I try to hide
beneath
a bricked-out
street light,
my back
against a wall,
waiting for a lie.

I know
there's no way
the night
will end well,
even if I get
what it is
I'm searching for,
relief
in the shape
of doom.

Solitary Self-Confinement

The longer
you're out here,
the more
bodies
stack up
around you.

Faces
come and go,
passing
you by
on their way
to an early
grave.

Don't get
comfortable
killing time
with someone,
don't rely
on mutual
understanding
of shared
experience
or shared drugs.

It all disappears,
eventually.

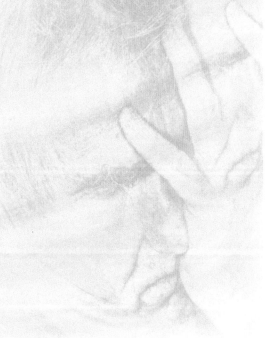

Not fit for Consumption

How many times
can a man
sell his soul
'till it becomes
recycled goods
un-fit
for landfills
or rats'
consumption?

I'm worried
I've reached
my limit.

With the shape
mine's in,
even the devil
won't barter
with me.

Destined to Float

A complicated game
of treading water
with my head
submerged.

The oxygen
increasingly
vacant,
causing
hyper-ventilation
to set the pace
in my head.

Flashes of light
amid the darkness
of closed eyelids
prove
I've no clue
how to swim
in this current
fighting me,
or am I
fighting
it?

Either way,
I'm pretty sure
I'm about to float.

Skewed Thinking

Sometimes
hard luck
and loaded dice
are birthright.

Sometimes
their tangents of self-
fulfilling prophecy
enticing death.

Sometimes
you can't tell
the difference.

Reasons
for competing
against yourself
in a blind race
to the grave
are woven
around bones.

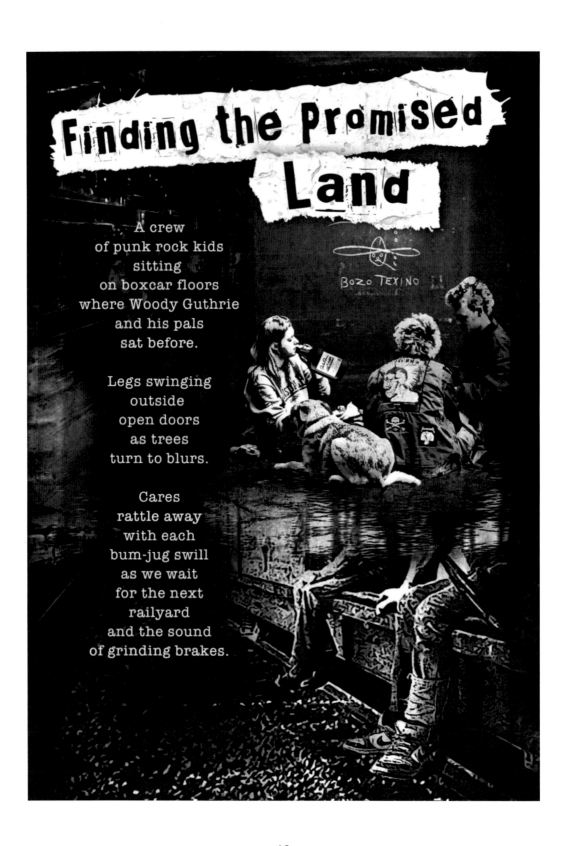

Finding the Promised Land

A crew
of punk rock kids
sitting
on boxcar floors
where Woody Guthrie
and his pals
sat before.

Legs swinging
outside
open doors
as trees
turn to blurs.

Cares
rattle away
with each
bum-jug swill
as we wait
for the next
railyard
and the sound
of grinding brakes.

Tragic Embrace

Wrapped
in the tragic
embrace
of an old lover's
track-marked arms.

Forsaking self
while lying
on linoleum,
oblivious
to the chaos
and content
with madness.

You give consent
by begging
for relief
found
in a spoonful
of illusion
laced with lies.

A midnight exchange
of disillusion
forsakes
everything
once held dear.

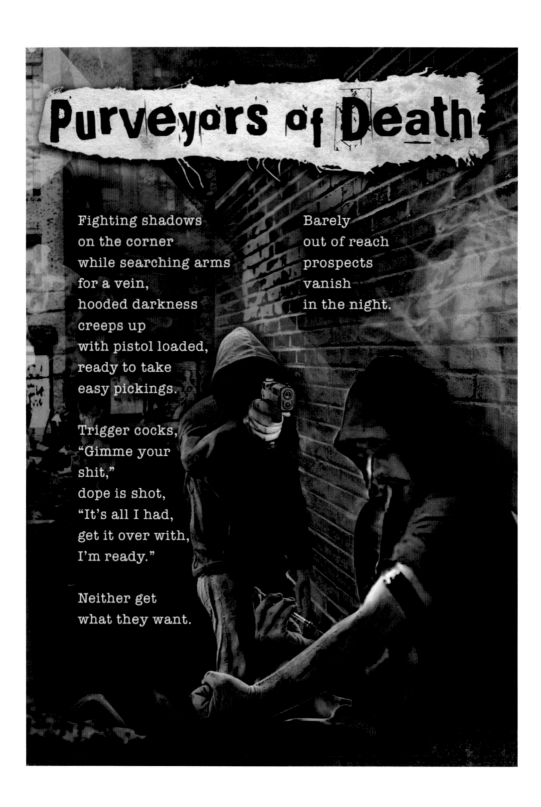

Purveyors of Death

Fighting shadows
on the corner
while searching arms
for a vein,
hooded darkness
creeps up
with pistol loaded,
ready to take
easy pickings.

Trigger cocks,
"Gimme your
shit,"
dope is shot,
"It's all I had,
get it over with,
I'm ready."

Neither get
what they want.

Barely
out of reach
prospects
vanish
in the night.

The Final Mind Eraser

A miscreant
propelling
poly-pharmic
misadventures
with multiple
altered mind states
that inhabit
the same space.

Each feeling
feeds the other
by keeping
your heart's
weaknesses
dulled.

Whoring self out
to an overload
of skewed thinking
that embraces
a soul's demise
and subdues
a pressure-cooked mind
with pin-pricked veins
and lazy eyes.

Slowly dying,
you relish
the thought
that peace
will be found
in something other
than chemical thieves
doing their best
to erase
the memories.

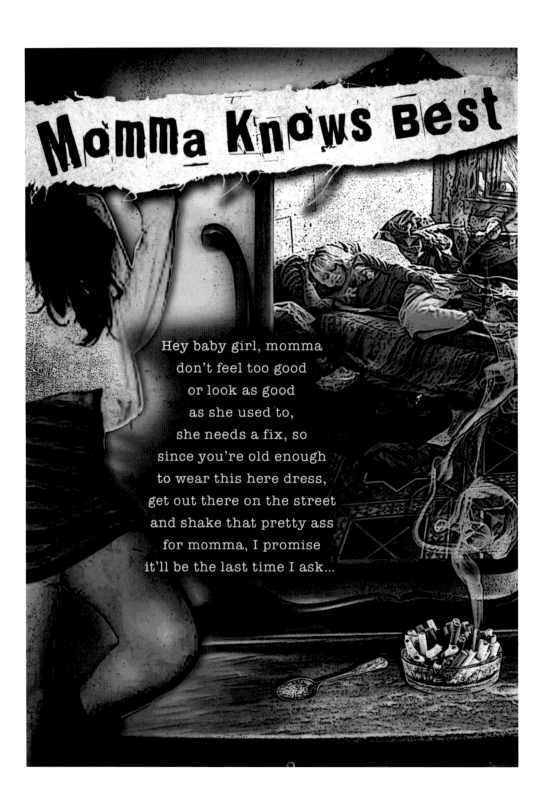

Momma Knows Best

Hey baby girl, momma
don't feel too good
or look as good
as she used to,
she needs a fix, so
since you're old enough
to wear this here dress,
get out there on the street
and shake that pretty ass
for momma, I promise
it'll be the last time I ask...

Zen and the Art of Pimping Your Girlfriend

(for Bloody)

As she goes
up the street
with a john
and turns
to walk down
an alley
where she
can fuck
and suck him
to a state
of nirvana,
repeat to yourself—
no attachment,
no attachment,
no attachment;
possession
keeps us separate
from enlightenment.

Just sayin'

If Cisco
is your
cologne,
gun oil
your
mouthwash,
Xanax
breakfast,
and you can't
effectively
kill yourself
no matter
how hard
you try,
it's time
to find
a new
strategy.

Squatting in Silence

I've searched
for darkness
in daylight.

I've sharpened
blades
on spines
of the lost
just to carve
redemption
from my heart.

Tonight
I'll be alone,
bleeding
on abandoned
floorboards.

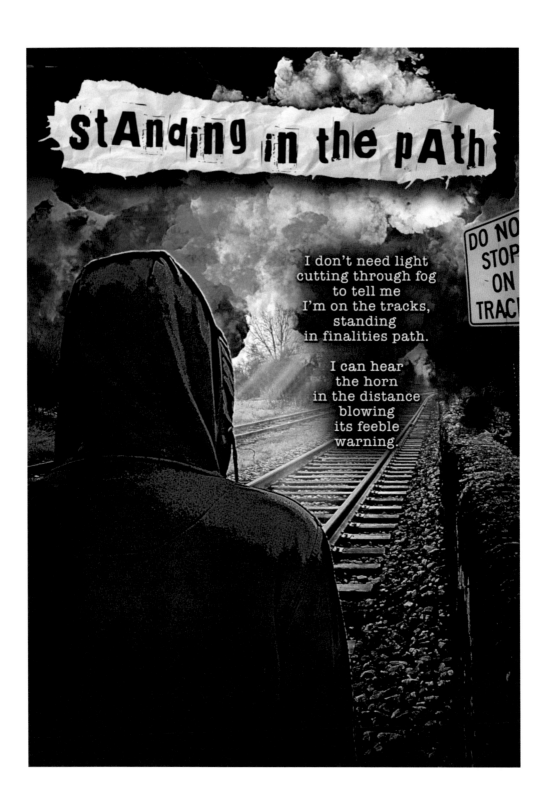

stAnding in the pAth

I don't need light
cutting through fog
to tell me
I'm on the tracks,
standing
in finalities path.

I can hear
the horn
in the distance
blowing
its feeble
warning.

DO NO
STOP
ON
TRAC

It's Not That Confusing Why

People
are dropping
at a rapid rate,
losing stride
and taking
their own lives.

I could
make a list
of names
but that would be
a book unto itself,
highlighting
last feelings.

I've got
more respect
for the dead
than I do
the living.

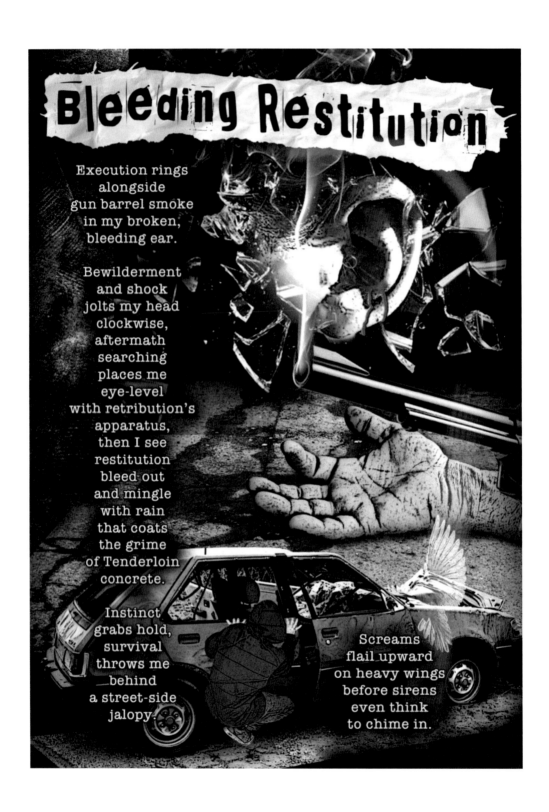

Bleeding Restitution

Execution rings
alongside
gun barrel smoke
in my broken,
bleeding ear.

Bewilderment
and shock
jolts my head
clockwise,
aftermath
searching
places me
eye-level
with retribution's
apparatus,
then I see
restitution
bleed out
and mingle
with rain
that coats
the grime
of Tenderloin
concrete.

Instinct
grabs hold,
survival
throws me
behind
a street-side
jalopy.

Screams
flail upward
on heavy wings
before sirens
even think
to chime in.

ExpenSive bEER

She thought Safeway
on Hawthorne
was a free store,
but lacked the mob
to prove it.

When she walked out
with a case of Beast Ice,
security was determined
to prove her wrong.

Martha's smiley swung
across his skull,
its lullaby spilled
from above his ear
onto the sidewalk.

For that, and a case
of schwag beer,
she got 2 years.

I was across town
either selling weed,
shooting dope,
begging for change,
or getting drunk.

It's hard to say which.

This is My Paradise, Lost

When you've got no place to go,
possessing secret betrayals of self
while roaming streets and alleyways,
your mind seems to wander
much further than your body
could ever possibly dream of going.

Unnoticed

When I'm gone
these streets
won't weep.

It will be as if
I never existed.

A new face
will replace mine —
begging for change,
eating trash,
drinking in alleys,
living on the skids.

I will remain
forever faceless,
just like the rest
of these poor
sons of bitches
who never
get noticed.

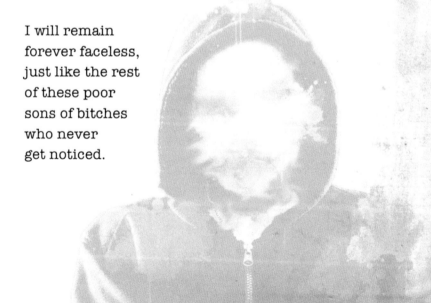

FiNAL Road Trip

His parked car running
on a back forty street
with garden hose connecting
tailpipe to window.

A woman walks by, mumbling,
"The things people do
just to get high."

He waves goodbye.

Suicide Note from A Habitual Bomb Maker

My own worst
enemy
is in my head,
creating scenes
of riotous
self-will
running
through streets.

A creature
of bad habit;
a good example
of bad ideas
blowing up
in unsuspecting
faces.

The scars
of evidence
are thick
on the heart
of everyone
who dared
love me.

Out With A Bang

Gutter went mad
after eating
lemon drop
Quaaludes
for months,
decided
to go out
with a bang.

Biting down
on a grenade,
he pulled
the pin.

Blowing off both
his head
and the roof
of the house
he lived in.

Scott Wozniak is a poet/chaos enthusiast living in Oregon. His work is widely published both online and in print. Other books he's written include, Crumbling Utopian Pipedream (Moran Press), Killing Our Saints (Svensk Apache Press), and Ash on Your Face like War Paint (Analog Submission Press).

Andrew Nutini is a freelance graphic artist living in Colorado and working under the name Found Image Design. His passion lies in splicing and rearranging images into striking new imagery. You can see more of his work at foundimagedesign.com.

Made in the USA
Lexington, KY
03 December 2019